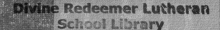
GOING TO SCHOOL
DURING THE
GREAT DEPRESSION

by Kerry A. Graves

Consultant: Jonathan J. Bean
Associate Professor of History, Southern Illinois University

Blue Earth Books

an imprint of Capstone Press
Mankato, Minnesota

Blue Earth Books are published by Capstone Press
151 Good Counsel Drive, P.O. Box 669, Mankato, Minnesota 56002
http://www.capstone-press.com

Library of Congress Cataloging-in-Publication Data
Graves, Kerry A.
    Going to school during the Great Depression / by Kerry A. Graves.
    p. cm.—(Going to school in history)
    Includes bibliographical references (p. 31) and index.
    ISBN 0-7368-0800-0
    1. Education—United States—History—20th century—Juvenile literature. 2. Depressions—1929—United States—Juvenile literature.
[1. Education—History—20th century. 2. Depressions—1929.] I. Title. II. Series.
    LA216 .G83 2002
    370'.973--dc21
                                                                                          00-013190

    Summary: Discusses school life during the Great Depression, including schools, lessons, books, and teachers. Addresses social and
economic life during the 1930s. Includes activities and sidebars.

Editorial Credits
Editor: Rachel Koestler
Designer and illustrator: Heather Kindseth
Product planning editor: Lois Wallentine
Photo researchers: Heidi Schoof and Judy Winter

Photo Credits
North Wind Picture Archives, cover; Bettmann/CORBIS, 11 (top), 16,
26; National Archives, 21, 27 (top); CORBIS, 3 (top), 19 (bottom), 22;
Special Collections Divisions, University of Washington Libraries/Lee, 5;
Franklin D. Roosevelt Library, 11 (bottom), 25; Library of Congress, 7,
19 (top), 20, 28, 29; Hulton Getty/Archive Photos, 6, 8; Arthur
Rothstein/CORBIS, 12, 23; Gregg Andersen, 17 (all); Seattle Public
Schools Archives, #223-161, 3 (bottom) 15 (top); Private Collection,
15 (bottom)

1 2 3 4 5 6 07 06 05 04 03 02

Contents

The Roaring Twenties to the Great Depression

During the 1920s, the United States' economy flourished. Many American businesses made large profits manufacturing automobiles and electrical appliances such as washing machines, refrigerators, and vacuum cleaners. Companies hired many workers to make these new products. With most Americans working, families could afford to buy homes, take trips, and go to the movies. People called these years the "Roaring Twenties."

The good times of the 1920s were the result of investments in the stock market. Beginning in the early 1900s, many business owners invested money in the New York Stock Exchange. About 1.5 million people spent their savings to buy stocks as well. Some people even borrowed money from banks to make their investments. As businesses became successful, they shared part of their profits with their shareholders. The value of successful business stocks also increased. As values rose, shareholders could sell their stocks for a profit.

But by 1929, economists were warning people that the stock market was not stable. They believed that stock values would eventually drop because stocks were priced high above their actual values. In mid-October 1929, stock prices began to drop. Investors began selling their stocks. They traded more than 12 million shares of stock on one single day, October 24. By Tuesday, October 29, 1929, shareholders had sold

When the stock market crashed, investors went from rich to poor overnight. Many people lost their homes. They built homemade shacks in neighborhoods called "Hoovervilles."

28 million shares of stock. The rapid sales activity caused the stock market to crash. People called this day Black Tuesday.

Stock prices dropped extremely low because there were more sellers than buyers. Many people had to sell their stocks for much less than they had paid for them. They could not afford to pay back the money they had borrowed to buy the stocks in the first place.

Stockholders went from rich to poor overnight. Some banks had used their customers' money to give loans to stock investors. The banks went broke when the investors could not pay back their loans. People rushed to banks to withdraw their savings. These bank runs caused many banks to run out of cash. Some banks had already closed. Millions of people lost their entire savings.

Buying Stocks

When a person buys stock in a company, they own a part of the company. Stocks are divided into portions called shares, which can be bought for a certain price. People who buy shares are called stockholders or shareholders. When a company does well, the value of the stock goes up, and the shares are worth more. If a company does poorly, the value of the shares goes down.

Shareholders can make a profit by selling stocks when the value goes up. People often hire brokers to buy and sell stocks for them. These professionals work at stock exchanges. Stockbrokers also give advice to people on which stocks to buy. Buying stocks often is risky. People sometimes lose money on stocks.

On Black Tuesday in 1929, people crowded outside the New York Stock Exchange on Wall Street.

When people realized they had lost their savings, they tried to save money. They stopped buying new products. Businesses had to cut back on production because they could not sell as many products. Many factories and stores shortened employees' working hours. Some businesses turned away workers because there was not enough work to do. Unemployed people could not pay their bills. Many families sold their homes, cars, and other possessions just to buy enough food.

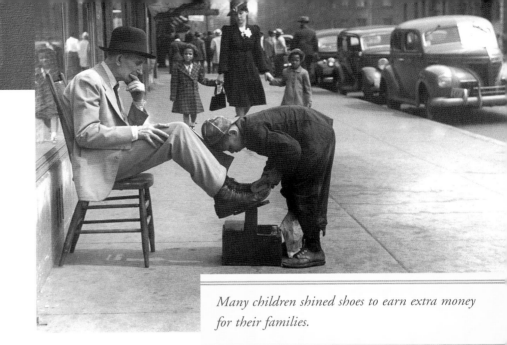

Many children shined shoes to earn extra money for their families.

The stock market crash affected people across the country and all over the world. U.S. banks could not afford to invest in foreign businesses. People were not buying imported products, and companies could not sell goods to foreign countries. In the United States, one in four people was unemployed. By 1932, almost 55 thousand businesses had closed. By 1933, more than 9,000 banks had failed. This time of economic crisis was called the Great Depression.

The U.S. government was not prepared to deal with the widespread poverty. President Herbert Hoover felt the government should stay out of people's personal lives. Hoover wanted people to work hard to solve their financial problems. He did not want citizens to become dependent on government aid. But U.S. leaders also realized many people needed help. They wanted private charities such as the Red Cross or local food shelters to provide families with help.

Instead, Hoover loaned money to large businesses. He believed that when these companies were again successful, owners could rehire workers at a good wage. He thought when

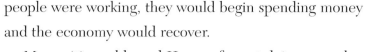

HOOVER'S
POOR FARM
TOBACCO
FUND

HARD TIMES ARE STILL
HOOVER ING OVER US

By 1932, people were upset that President Herbert Hoover had not done more to end the Great Depression.

people were working, they would begin spending money and the economy would recover.

Many citizens blamed Hoover for not doing enough to help them out of poverty. People who lost their homes often lived in shacks made from cardboard and scrap metal. They called neighborhoods of these shacks "Hoovervilles." Homeless people who wrapped themselves in newspapers to keep warm said they were sleeping with "Hoover blankets." In the 1932 presidential election, citizens showed their dislike for Hoover by electing Franklin D. Roosevelt as their new president.

During the Great Depression, parents of large families often struggled to feed their children. Older children looked for work, but most could not find jobs. Some left home so the family would have fewer mouths to feed. These young people went to larger cities or traveled west in search of work. They jumped into the cargo cars of moving trains, "riding the rails" to anywhere they could find work.

Many families worked together to survive. Some children dropped out of school to care for younger siblings while their parents worked or looked for jobs. Many children took up jobs shining shoes, selling newspapers, and working in clothing mills.

Traveling Route 66

Legend	
—— Route 66	
dust bowl region	
Great Plains region	

During the 1930s, the southern Great Plains experienced drought. Because the soil was dry, strong winds picked up dust and carried it into the air. So many of these dust storms hit the southern Great Plains region that people called this area the dust bowl. Dust storms continued to hit the Great Plains for five years.

Farmers experienced hard times. Crops did not grow because there was not enough rainfall. Farmers lost money and were unable to pay their mortgages. Banks foreclosed on farmland. Many farm families left the Great Plains and moved west in search of work. They packed their belongings into their cars, or jalopies, and strapped mattresses to the roof. They drove on Route 66 through Texas, New Mexico, and Arizona. They crossed the Black Mountains and the Mojave Desert on their way into southern California. Jalopies sometimes broke down along the way or overheated in the desert. Families then grabbed what they could carry and began walking.

Schools in the Thirties

In the early 1900s, the type of school that students attended depended on where they lived. Children who lived in or near cities went to large public schools. In rural areas, most children went to classes in a one-room schoolhouse.

During the first years of the Great Depression, city classrooms often were crowded. In order to save money, many school districts hired fewer teachers. Classrooms often did not have enough desks for every student. There were not enough books and supplies for the entire class.

In the early 1900s, schools used money received from property taxes to buy books and supplies and to pay teachers' salaries. As people began to lose their jobs, they were unable to pay taxes on their property. Public schools received less funding each year.

Some schools shortened their terms to save money. In some states, schools opened for only 60 days the entire year. Many schools cut kindergarten classes and did not rehire school nurses. Instead, they saved money for supplies and building repairs.

School districts could not afford new books. In 1932, there were one million more students in school than there were in 1930. But textbook purchases were down 30 percent. Many young readers were forced to used damaged books that often had pages missing. Some classes were canceled if the books could not be replaced. Many schools could not afford to purchase up-to-date materials. School districts cut special classes such as home economics, physical education, art, and foreign languages. Teachers held classes for just the basic "three Rs"—reading, writing, and arithmetic.

During the Great Depression, schools began to require that students bring their own classroom supplies, paper, and pencils. Some parents could not afford these supplies and had to stop sending their children to school. Many students did not have nice clothes or shoes to wear. Their clothing was torn and worn out. Many children dropped out of school because they did not have proper clothes to wear.

In urban areas, children attended large public schools (above). Rural children went to school in one-room schoolhouses (below).

11

Rural students walked or rode their bicycles to school.

"With the school closed (I feel like crying every time I see it with the doors and windows boarded up) I'll be too old before I'm ready to go to high school. Do you think that you could get on without a school or even a set of books? Grace has the Arithmetic VIII and I have the Grammar. Teacher let us borrow these books when school closed. I guess she had a hunch how this year was going to be."

—a 14-year-old farm girl writes to a friend, from **Riding the Rails**

Children often felt a lot of pressure to do well in school. Many parents looked to their children's education to pull them out of their financial burdens. They hoped their children would get a good job after finishing school.

Advertisers often used the parable of the Unraised Hand to sell their products. In these advertisements for cereal, vitamins, or other products, a student who did not have the product was shown in a classroom. The students around the child all had their hands raised to answer the teacher's question. The one child who did not have the product sat slumped in the desk with both arms down. Advertisers hoped parents would buy the product to help their child be a better student.

By 1933, many public schools had closed because of low funding. These school closings left about 3 million children in the United States without the opportunity to go to school.

Teachers

School districts hired more female teachers during the Great Depression than they had in the 1800s. In the early 1900s, female teachers earned less than male teachers. School districts saved money by hiring female teachers.

During the early 1900s, urban public school districts began to require teachers to have normal school training. Normal schools were teacher colleges that offered training in classroom organization and teaching methods. During the Great Depression, most school districts paid teachers a flat fee, regardless of education or experience.

Most rural schoolteachers had only a high school diploma. The local school board interviewed teachers to test their knowledge. During interviews, teachers answered questions about various subjects and teaching methods. Many rural schoolteachers were 16 years old when they began teaching.

School districts around the country cut costs to keep their schools open. They often cut teachers' salaries. Some districts paid their teachers in scrip. These paper slips listed an amount of money the school owed the teacher. Teachers took scrip payments to local stores and exchanged them for food and other items.

More than 7,000 teachers lost their jobs during the Great Depression. In some counties, teachers worked for a room and food, with no additional pay at all. Some rural schoolteachers lived in the schoolhouse and cooked their meals on the wood-burning stove.

City Schools

Most children in cities attended public grammar schools. Students started grammar school at age 5 or 6. Teachers separated students into grades according to their age. Classrooms ranged from 30 to 50 students. Hundreds of children often attended grammar schools. In some large cities, school districts built junior high schools or middle schools. Students attended these schools after completing grammar school at about age 12. Junior high schools prepared students for high school.

City schools were large brick buildings with many classrooms. By the 1930s, most public schools had electric lights, central heating, and running water for sinks, toilets, and drinking fountains. Students sat at individual desks, which were placed in rows.

In grammar school, children studied reading, writing, arithmetic, spelling, and geography. Students also took classes in art, music, and physical education. Teachers recorded students' grades twice each semester and sent the report cards home to parents. Teachers also graded their students on citizenship and behavior.

Children learned to read from *The Elson Readers*. These books taught reading through simple stories about a boy named Dick and girl named Jane. Teachers used an over-sized version of the readers titled *Our Big Book*. *Our Big Book* came with an

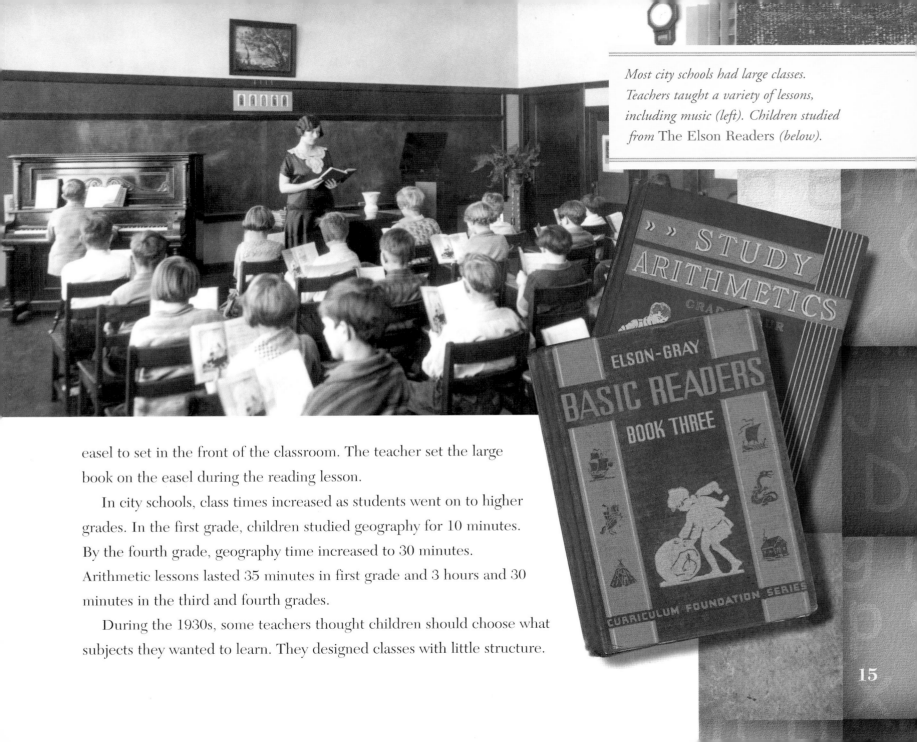

Most city schools had large classes.
Teachers taught a variety of lessons,
including music (left). Children studied
from The Elson Readers (below).

easel to set in the front of the classroom. The teacher set the large
book on the easel during the reading lesson.

In city schools, class times increased as students went on to higher
grades. In the first grade, children studied geography for 10 minutes.
By the fourth grade, geography time increased to 30 minutes.
Arithmetic lessons lasted 35 minutes in first grade and 3 hours and 30
minutes in the third and fourth grades.

During the 1930s, some teachers thought children should choose what
subjects they wanted to learn. They designed classes with little structure.

In these progressive classrooms, teachers encouraged students to discover their own interests. Students were free to read, play, and ask teachers questions about books and other materials.

Progressive classrooms often were arranged in a casual way. Instead of placing desks in rows, teachers sometimes used moveable desks or long tables and chairs. This arrangement allowed students freedom to move around the classroom and be more comfortable while they worked on assignments. Some teachers added window curtains, rugs, or stuffed chairs and sofas to their rooms to make them seem more like home.

Progressive teachers spent little time lecturing from textbooks. Students often worked in small groups. They completed art and science projects, learned to sing and dance, and went on field trips.

Many parents disliked progressive teaching methods. They wanted their children to spend school time on basic subjects, such as reading, writing, and arithmetic. Some progressive schools did not use regular textbooks, give homework, or assign letter grades. Progressive teachers wanted students to be excited about going to school. But parents often feared that children who attended progressive schools would not work hard in class or at home.

In progressive schools, students spent little time studying from textbooks. They learned lessons in creative ways.

16

Make Tin Can Stompers

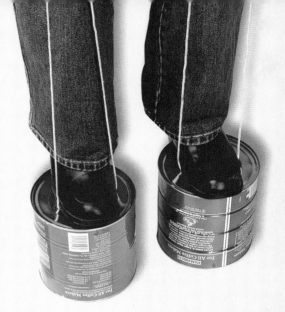

During the Great Depression, families often could not afford to buy toys. Many children made homemade toys, such as rag dolls, wooden toy soldiers, and tin can stompers.

What You Need

2 empty coffee cans

bottle opener

thin rope or twine, about 16 feet (5 meters) long

tape measure

scissors

What You Do

1. On a flat surface, turn the cans upside down.
2. Use the pointed side of the bottle opener to punch two holes in the bottom of each can. Punch one hole about 2 inches (5 centimeters) from the edge of the can. Punch another hole directly across from the first hole on the other side of the bottom. The hole needs to be big enough to fit the rope or twine through it.
3. Take the rope or twine and measure a length from your waist to the floor. Double this length, add about 6 inches (15 centimeters), and cut. Cut a second length of rope the same length. These will be your stomper handles.

4. Thread the ends of the ropes down through the holes in the bottom of the can. Carefully pull them through and tie the ends together to keep the rope from pulling back through the hole. Then pull the rope back through the can until the knots are against the inside bottom of the can.
5. Carefully place your feet between the rope loops and stand on bottoms of the cans. Pull up on the handles until the ropes are tight to steady yourself. Lift the ropes as you walk on your stompers.

Dust Bowl Schools

Schools in rural areas were very different from city schools. Children who lived in rural areas often went to a one-room schoolhouse. Most of these schools did not have electricity or running water. A blackboard usually covered the front wall. Some schoolhouses had rows of individual or double desks. Other schools had long benches with desk tops built into the back of each row. One-room schoolhouses had wood or coal stoves for heat and lanterns for light. Students took drinks from an outdoor water pump.

Students in rural areas often lived far away from school. Some rural children walked several miles to school each day. Other students rode bicycles or horses. Some rural towns used a farm wagon for a bus. Farm wagon buses had an enclosed truck bed with benches lining either side of the bed.

Rural schools were small. They often had only one or two teachers. Students of all ages sat together in the classroom. Classes held between 20 to 60 students, depending on how many families lived in the area.

Rural schoolteachers taught all subjects through eighth grade. Teachers spent about five and a half to six hours a day instructing students. Students recited their homework to the teacher. During recitations, teachers asked students questions as a group and individually. Students sometimes read aloud and explained passages from their textbooks. Recitations lasted about 10 to 15 minutes. When the teacher felt students understood the lesson, he or she assigned the next pages in the textbook. While one grade was giving their recitation, students in the other grades studied their subjects individually at their seats or worked on math problems at the blackboard.

Children who lived on farms did not attend school regularly. They often helped with spring planting and fall harvesting. Many parents felt the family farmwork was more important than school. During these busy times, children attended school part-time or quit until the work was finished. Many children fed the farm animals, helped milk the cows, or finished other chores before they left for school each morning. Children often quit school after eighth grade and began working full-time on the farm.

Rural schools did not have indoor plumbing. Children often took drinks from a water pump (above). At school, they learned reading, writing, and arithmetic (below).

19

In 1930 and 1931, farm families on the Great Plains had bumper wheat crops. These large crops caused a surplus of wheat. Wheat prices dropped because people were buying less and warehouses were full. When farmers did not have money to pay their mortgages, many banks foreclosed on their farms. People began moving west in search of work.

Between 1931 and 1936, the Great Plains experienced drought. Farmers depended on rainfall to help their crops grow. The dry topsoil made farming difficult. Wheat plants did not hold the topsoil firmly in the ground.

On April 14, 1935, a day known as Black Sunday, a dust storm hit Kansas. High winds carried large amounts of topsoil, causing a

Gaycats and Dingbats

During the Great Depression, more than 250,000 boys and girls, ages 8 to 18, left their homes. Many of them hoped to find work and send money home to their families. Fathers and sons sometimes rode the rails together. Other children ran away so their families would have one less person to feed. People often called these runaways "hoboes."

Hoboes rode the rails from city to city. They jumped into moving cargo train cars to avoid paying for a train ticket. Most hoboes did not carry many personal belongings. They sometimes carried a blanket or a change of clothes in a cloth sack. Hoboes sometimes joined a push. This group of teenagers rode the rails together.

Gaycats, or new hoboes, needed to learn how to ride the rails safely. Many young gaycats died jumping on and off trains. In time, gaycats became dingbats, or experienced hoboes. Some cities had small villages of hoboes called jungles.

Riding the rails was dangerous. Many hoboes became injured or died jumping on and off moving trains.

large black cloud of dust to blow through Kansas towns. During the next five years, many dust storms hit the Great Plains region. People began calling the southern Plains region the "dust bowl."

Drought and dust storms forced many families to leave their farms. Families who traveled west to California in search of work were called migrants. Many migrants tried to find work on farms. But after traveling many miles, some migrants discovered that jobs were scarce. Migrant families often lived out of their cars or in tents. When money ran out, some families sold their belongings, cars, and tents in order to buy food.

Californians called migrants "Okies" because many of them came from Oklahoma. Okies often were treated poorly just because they wore old clothing and talked with a southern accent.

After months of traveling, Okie children were behind in school lessons. Many children did not know how to read or write. California schools

Dust particles rubbing in the air caused so much static electricity that cars shorted out. People often received shocks when they touched metal objects.

Some migrant children worked as field pickers.

were more advanced than schools in the dust bowl. Children who were placed in a grade based on their age were not ready for the harder lessons. Teachers sometimes thought the children were unable to learn. In schools, teachers often made Okie students sit on the floor. Schoolteachers considered Okie accents a speech defect. They placed Okie students in special speech programs to teach them to speak without an accent.

Migrant children were ashamed that they were poor. Other children sometimes teased them because of their torn clothing. Some students walked home instead of taking a bus so their classmates would not know that they lived in tents. Instead of bringing sandwiches for lunch, Okie children brought cornbread or biscuits and beans.

New Deal Schools

President Franklin Roosevelt created many programs to help Americans during the Great Depression. During his presidency, families listened to "fireside chats." In these frequent radio programs, Roosevelt explained his plans for economic recovery. He called his plans to end the Great Depression the "New Deal."

The New Deal established government agencies to create jobs for Americans. The Civilian Conservation Corps, or CCC, hired people to plant trees in parks, clear campgrounds, and build dams. President Roosevelt also started the Civil Works Administration (CWA), the Public Works Administration (PWA), and the Works Progress Administration (WPA). These agencies hired people to build schools, hospitals, roads, bridges, and playgrounds. People called New Deal organizations alphabet agencies because the names often were abbreviated into three letters.

Some New Deal programs helped children and teenagers. The WPA provided money to schools to hire teachers and pay for supplies. Through the WPA, First Lady Eleanor Roosevelt set up a hot lunch program in schools. Public schools provided free hot lunches to more than 119,000 needy students every day. These meals included a hot dish, sandwiches, a piece of fruit or pudding, and milk.

The government provided money to build and repair thousands of schools. School districts received funding to hire teachers and reopen schools. Through government projects, PWA and WPA crews also built cafeterias, auditoriums, laboratories, libraries, and gymnasiums.

New Deal programs reduced overcrowding in public schools. Program workers added classrooms to rural schools or built larger schools to replace the many one-room schoolhouses. With larger schools, teachers could organize classes into grades. They had more time to work with individual students. Separated grades helped students receive a better education.

Government funding also began providing school bus transportation to students. Children who lived far away from school could attend more easily.

The government also established federal camps for migrant workers. In these camps,

First Lady Eleanor Roosevelt helped set up a hot lunch program in public schools. This lunch program provided children with a nutritious meal every day.

Dear Mrs. Roosevelt

Young people in the United States looked to Eleanor Roosevelt to solve their problems of poverty. Many children wrote her letters asking for money, clothing, and other necessities. Some children asked for shoes, dresses, or bikes so they could go to school. Other children asked for medical help. Eleanor Roosevelt could not write back to all of these children. But she tried to help them by creating federal youth programs.

Eleanor Roosevelt wanted homeless children to stay in school. During the 1930s, she urged Congress to establish the National Youth Administration, or NYA. The NYA helped older students stay in school by offering them grants in exchange for work. Students worked in libraries and on farms in exchange for an education. Eleanor Roosevelt also helped create nutrition programs and recreation programs in public schools.

Eleanor Roosevelt is shown at breakfast with a group of students in a progressive school.

The National Youth Administration (NYA) was part of the Works Progress Administration (WPA). This agency organized work programs for youths that offered training in various trades.

families paid one dollar a week for a one-room cabin or a tent. If they did not have the money to pay for rent, they could work at the camp in exchange for housing. One of these camps was Weedpatch Camp, near Bakersfield, California.

In 1940, Leo Hart opened a school for migrant children at Weedpatch Camp. Hart hoped that children would not only get a good education, but would feel better about themselves without the cruelty of teachers and other local students. In addition to basic subjects, such as reading, writing, and arithmetic, Weedpatch School offered courses in various trades. Teachers held classes in plumbing, carpentry, and electrical wiring.

Weedpatch School had a unique plan of study. Students studied agriculture and planted their own gardens. They grew foods such as potatoes, alfalfa, tomatoes, corn, carrots, and watermelons. Cooks used these foods to prepare school lunches. Weedpatch School also had its own livestock pens. Students learned how to feed, raise, and butcher animals. The principal at Weedpatch School

The Red Cross helped people during the Great Depression by distributing food to needy families.

bought a C-46 airplane to instruct students in aircraft mechanics. If students kept a 90 percent grade in arithmetic, they got to drive the plane down a makeshift runway.

Even though the New Deal helped many people find jobs, the Great Depression lasted through the 1930s. In 1941, the United States entered World War II (1939–1945) against Germany, Italy, and Japan. Many factories reopened to build supplies for the U.S. Military. Millions of men and women went back to work to build planes and ships and to make weapons, ammunition, uniforms, and other products. With people back at work, the economy recovered. The United States' involvement in World War II helped bring an end to the Great Depression.

Organize a Food Drive

During the Great Depression, people often depended on soup kitchens or other charities for food (right). Today, there are still many people who are unable to feed their families. You can help hungry families by donating food to a local food bank. This can be a great community service project for your school. You will need a teacher or other adult to help organize your food drive.

What You Need

poster board
pens, markers, or crayons
one or more large boxes for each classroom to hold food items

What You Do

1. With your teacher, choose a local food bank. Your teacher should contact this group to find out about the acceptable types of food and other donation guidelines.
2. Set a start and end date for your food drive. One week usually is enough time.
3. Invite other classes to join you in your food drive. You could hold a contest to see which class brings the most cans or packages of food.
4. Each class needs its own food box.
5. Create colorful posters to place around your school to remind people to bring food. Be sure to list the start and end dates for the contest.
6. During the week of your food drive, encourage everyone to bring in cans and boxes of food. Each class should place their food in their own box and watch it fill up during the week.
7. On the last day of your food drive, each class should count their food items. Your teacher should double-check your total. Compare classes to see who brought the most food. Add all the class totals together for a grand total amount.
8. Your teacher or parent volunteers can drop the donations off at the food bank.

Words to Know

bumper (BUHM-pur)—large or abundant

depression (di-PRESH-uhn)—a time when businesses do poorly and people lose money; the American Great Depression lasted from 1929–1941.

economist (i-KON-uh-mist)—someone who studies the way money, goods, and services are used in a society

migrant (MYE-gruhnt)—someone who moves from place to place doing seasonal labor

normal school (NOR-muhl SKOOL)—a teacher's training college

rural (RUR-uhl)—an area in the countryside or outside of the city

scrip (SKRIP)—a paper receipt with a written amount owed to an employee; teachers used scrip payments to buy items at local stores during the Great Depression.

stock (STOK)—a piece of a company that is sold to investors; a person who buys stock invests money in a company and owns a part of it.

stockholder (STOK-hohl-dur)—a person who owns stocks, or shares, in a company

To Learn More

Nishi, **Dennis.** *Life During the Great Depression*. The Way People Live. San Diego: Lucent Books, 1998.

Ross, **Stewart.** *The Great Depression: Causes and Consequences*. Causes and Consequences. Austin, Texas: Raintree Steck-Vaughn, 1998.

Stein, **R. Conrad.** *The Great Depression*. Cornerstones of Freedom. Chicago: Children's Press, 1993.

Woog, **Adam.** *Roosevelt and the New Deal*. World History Series. San Diego: Lucent Books, 1998.

Internet Sites

The Day of the Black Blizzard
http://www.discovery.com/area/history/dustbowl/
   dustbowlopener.html

Franklin D. Roosevelt National Historic Site
http://www.nps.gov/hofr/hofrhome.html

The New Deal Network
http://newdeal.feri.org/classrm/links.htm

Voices from the Dust Bowl
http://lcweb2.loc.gov/ammem/afctshtml/tshome.html

Weedpatch Camp
http://www.netxn.com/~weedpatch

Places to Visit

Center for New Deal Studies
Roosevelt University
430 South Michigan Avenue
Chicago, IL 60605

Civilian Conservation Corps Museum
North Higgins Lake State Park
11747 North Higgins Lake Drive
Roscommon, MI 48653-8448

Herbert Hoover Presidential Library and Museum
210 Parkside Drive
West Branch, IA 52358-9685

New York Stock Exchange
Interactive Education Center
20 Broad Street, 3rd Floor
New York, NY 10005

Index